# The GIFT of FATHER CHRISTMAS

## STORIES and TRADITIONS of ST. NICHOLAS

### D. Morgan

HARVEST HOUSE PUBLISHERS

EUGENE, OREGON

THE GIFT OF FATHER CHRISTMAS
Text Copyright © 2002 by Harvest House Publishers
Eugene, Oregon 97402

Library of Congress Cataloging-in-Publication Data

The gift of Father Christmas / artwork by D. Morgan.
   p. cm.
 ISBN 0-7369-0571-5 (alk. paper)
 1. Christmas--Literary collections. 1. Morgan, D. (Doris)
 PN6071.C6 G54 2002
 808.8'0334--dc21

          2002002886

Design and production by Koechel Peterson and Associates, Minneapolis, Minnesota

Printed in China

02 03 04 05 06 07 08 09 10 / IM / 10 9 8 7 6 5 4 3 2

# The GIFT of FATHER CHRISTMAS

The spirit of Christmas is embodied in giving, sharing, and caring for those around you. From centuries past, one of the most inspirational figures who personifies all of these qualities and more is Father Christmas. Just the thought of him awakens a sense of wonder in kids and adults alike. From Holland to Harlem, his name is whispered on the lips of children all over the world. He is the keeper of dreams and harvester of hopes.

His story begins in what is now Turkey, early in the fourth century. Saint Nicholas grew up a devout Christian who dedicated his life to the poor and was known throughout the land for his generous spirit. Not wanting to bring attention to his good deeds, he chose to leave his gifts at night so they would go mostly unnoticed. He was appointed to the Council of Nicaea in A.D. 325 by Constantine of Rome and was later officially named the patron saint of children. His example of charitable giving soon spread all throughout Europe. The tradition of Saint Nicholas' good deeds was kept alive best by the Dutch. In sixteenth-century Holland, Dutch children would place their wooden shoes by the hearth in hopes that they would be filled with a treat. Their spelling of Saint Nicholas, Sint Nikolaas, eventually became Sinterklaas and is where we get our present-day name for him: Santa Claus. From these beginnings, some of our most beloved Christmas traditions were created.

So when the stockings are hung by the chimney with care in hopes that Saint Nicholas soon will be there, take a moment to remember what the true spirit of Father Christmas is all about.

Silent snow is falling, soft as Christmas prayer.
On this Holy night a host of angels there.

D. Morgan

"The spirit of a great Love is abroad in the
cold and the night, filling the empty, comforting
the comfortless, and smiling on the joy of little
children everywhere."
And when the children besought her to tell
them more of this shining Spirit, and of how he
seeks and finds rows of empty shoes in cottage
and in castle she told them of the bent old man,
muffled in his great coat of scarlet and fur, whom
she had seen with her own young eyes in the
castle court, and of how his silver beard glistened
in the moonlight, and of his jolly laugh when he
found the little shoes waiting to be filled.

FLORENCE MORSE KINGSLEY
"The First Coming"

Our hearts they hold all Christmas dear,

And earth seems sweet and heaven seems near.

MARJORIE PICKALL

The magi, as you know, were wise men—
wonderfully wise men—who brought gifts to the
Babe in the manger. They invented the art of
giving Christmas presents.

O. HENRY
The Gift of the Magi

*I will honor Christmas in my heart, and try to keep it all the year.*

CHARLES DICKENS

Anne's first Christmas in her own house
was as delightful as she could have wished.
The day was fine and bright; the first
skim of snow had fallen on Christmas
Eve and made the world beautiful; the
harbor was still open and glittering.

L.M. MONTGOMERY
*Anne's House of Dreams*

*May no gift be too small to give, nor too simple to receive,*
*which is wrapped in thoughtfulness, and tied with love.*

L.O. BAIRD

It is more blessed to give than to receive.

THE BOOK OF ACTS

Memories in the making

Candlelight for two ...

There's a little bit of magic

Coming

The manner of giving is worth more than the gift.

PIERRE CORNEILLE

*Charity should begin at home, but should not stay there.*

PHILLIPS BROOKS

I'd take the mother's fears away,
The doubts which often fret the wise—
And all should wake on Christmas Day
With happy hearts and shining eyes.

For old and young this is my prayer:
God bless us all this Christmas Day
And give us strength our tasks to bear,
And take our bitter griefs away!

EDGAR GUEST

*Kindness begets kindness.*

GREEK PROVERB

A man is at his finest towards the finish of the year;
He is almost what he should be when the Christmas season's here;
Then he's thinking more of others than he's thought the months before,
And the laughter of his children is a joy worth toiling for.
He is less a selfish creature than at any other time;
When the Christmas spirit rules him he comes close to the sublime.

When it's Christmas man is bigger and is better in his part;
He is keener for the service that is prompted by the heart.
All the petty thoughts and narrow seem to vanish for awhile
And the true reward he's seeking is the glory of a smile.
Then for others he is toiling and somehow it seems to me
That at Christmas he is almost what God wanted him to be.

If I had to paint a picture of a man I think I'd wait
Till he'd fought his selfish battles and had put aside his hate.
I'd not catch him at his labors when his thoughts are all of self,
On the long days and dreary when he's striving for himself.
I'd not take him when he's sneering, when he's scornful or depressed,
But I'd look for him at Christmas when he's shining at his best.

Man is ever in a struggle and he's oft misunderstood;
There are days the worst that's in him is the master of the good,
But at Christmas kindness rules him and he puts himself aside
And his petty hates are vanquished and his heart is opened wide.
Oh, I don't know how to say it, but somehow it seems to me
That at Christmas man is almost what God sent him here to be.

EDGAR GUEST.

Snow, however, began to thicken and fall fast; and Syme, having found one glance at the wax lady quite sufficient to depress his spirits, stared out instead into the white and empty street. He was considerably astonished to see, standing quite still outside the shop and staring into the window, a man. His top hat was loaded with snow like the hat of Father Christmas, the white drift was rising round his boots and ankles; but it seemed as if nothing could tear him away from the contemplation of the colourless wax doll in dirty evening dress. That any human being should stand in such weather looking into such a shop was a matter of sufficient wonder...

G.K. CHESTERTON
*The Man Who Was Thursday*

ow, Willie, you know we must firmly believe
That presents we ask for we're sure to receive.
You must wait just as still till I say amen.
And by that you will know that your turn has come then.—
Dear Jesus, look down on my brother and me,
And grant us the favor we're asking of thee:
I want a nice book full of pictures, a ring,
A writing desk, too, that shuts with a spring,
Bless papa, dear Jesus, and cause him to see
That Santa Claus loves us as much even as he;
Don't let him get fretful and angry again
At dear brother Willie and Annie, Amen!"

Their prayers being ended, they raised up their heads,
And with hearts light and cheerful again sought their beds;
They were soon lost in slumber—both peaceful and deep,
And with fairies in dreamland were roaming in sleep.

And then he softly ascended the stairs,
And arriving at their door heard both of their prayers
His Annie's "bless papa" draws forth the big tears,
And Willie's grave promise falls sweet on his ears.
"Strange, strange, I've forgotten," said he with a sigh
"How I longed when a child to have Christmas draw nigh.
I'll atone for my harshness," he inwardly said,
"By answering their prayers, ere I sleep in my bed..."

And he said to himself as he brushed off a tear,
"I'm happier tonight than I have been for a year...
Hereafter I'll make it a rule, I believe,
To have Santa Claus visit us each Christmas Eve."

So thinking he gently extinguished the light
And tripped down stairs to retire for the night.

As soon as the beams of the bright morning sun
Put the darkness to flight, and the stars one by one,
Four little blue eyes out of sleep opened wide,
And at the same moment the presents espied.
Then out of their beds they sprang with a bound,
And the very gifts prayed for were all of them found;
They laughed and they cried in their innocent glee,
And shouted for papa to come quick and see
What presents old Santa Claus had brought in the night
(Just the things they had wanted) and left before light.

"And now," said Annie, in a voice soft and low,
"You'll believe there's a Santa Claus, papa, I know";
While dear little Willie climbed up on his knee,
Determined no secret between them should be,
And told, in soft whispers, how Annie had said,
That their dear, blessed mama, so long ago dead
Used to kneel down and pray by the side of her chair,
And that God, up in heaven, had answered her prayer:
"Then we got up and prayed just as well as we could,
And God answered our prayers; now wasn't he good?"
"I should say that he was if he sent you all these,
And knew just what presents my children would please."
(Well, well, let him think so, the dear little elf,
'Twould be cruel to tell him I did it myself.)

Blind father, who caused your stern heart to relent?
And the hasty word spoken so soon to repent?
'Twas the Being who bade you steal softly up stairs,
And made you his agent to answer their prayers."

Sophia P. Snow
*"Annie and Willie's Prayer"*

Fame and fortune - father treasures - vanish fast - but with Present, Past and future . . . only Love will last

D. Morgan

Somehow not only for Christmas
But all the long year through,
The joy that you give others
Is the joy that comes back to you.

And the more you spend in blessing
The poor and lonely and sad,
The more of your heart's possessing
Returns to make you glad.

JOHN GREENLEAF WHITTIER

*I*t is good to be children sometimes, and never better than at Christmas, when its mighty Founder was a child Himself.

CHARLES DICKENS

Heap on more wood!—the wind is chill;
But let it whistle as it will
We'll keep our Christmas merry still.

SIR WALTER SCOTT

*F*ine old Christmas, with the snowy hair and ruddy face, had done his duty that year in the noblest fashion, and had set off his rich gifts of warmth and color with all the heightening contrast of frost and snow.

Snow lay on the croft and river-bank in undulations softer than the limbs of infancy; it lay with the neatliest finished border on every sloping roof, making the dark-red gables stand out with a new depth of color; it weighed heavily on the laurels and fir-trees, till it fell from them with a shuddering sound; it clothed the rough turnip-field with whiteness, and made the sheep look like dark blotches; the gates were all blocked up with the sloping drifts, and here and there a disregarded four-footed beast stood as if petrified "in unrecumbent sadness"; there was no gleam, no shadow, for the heavens, too, were one still, pale cloud; no sound or motion in anything but the dark river that flowed and moaned like an unresting sorrow. But old Christmas smiled as he laid this cruel-seeming spell on the outdoor world, for he meant to light up home with new brightness, to deepen all the richness of indoor color, and give a keener edge of delight to the warm fragrance of food; he meant to prepare a sweet imprisonment that would strengthen the primitive fellowship of kindred, and make the sunshine of familiar human faces as welcome as the hidden day-star. His kindness fell but hardly on the homeless,—fell but hardly on the homes where the hearth was not very warm, and where the food had little fragrance; where the human faces had had no sunshine in them, but rather the leaden, blank-eyed gaze of unexpectant want. But the fine old season meant well; and if he has not learned the secret how to bless men impartially, it is because his father Time, with ever-unrelenting purpose, still hides that secret in his own mighty, slow-beating heart.

GEORGE ELIOT
*The Mill on the Floss*

With every Christmas card I write

D. Morgan

*Each person has inside a basic decency and goodness.*
*If he listens to it and acts on it, he is giving a great deal*
*of what it is the world needs most. It is not complicated*
*but it takes courage...to listen to his own goodness.*

PABLO CASALS

Nothing happens.....

D. Morgan ©

..... Without a dream.

*Kindness is always fashionable.*

AMELIA E. BARR

# Merry Christmas Around the World

United States: Merry Christmas
Mexico: Feliz Navidad
France: Joyeux Noël
Holland: Vrolijk Kerstfeest
Germany: Froehliche Weihnachten
Italy: Buon Natale
Sweden: God Jul
Russia: S prazdnikom Rozhdestva
Afrikaans: Geséende Kerfees
Greek: Kala Christougenna
Hawaii: Mele Kalikimaka
Japan: Shinnen omedeto
China: Kung His Hsin Nien
Thailand: Suksan Wan Christmas

*It is only in the giving of oneself to others that we truly live.*

Ethel Percy Andrus

And it was always said of him that
he knew how to keep Christmas well,
if any man possessed the knowledge.
And so, as Tiny Tim observed,
God bless us, every one!

CHARLES DICKENS
*A Christmas Carol*

---

Her stocking by the chimney place
Gives to the room a touch of grace
More beautiful than works of art
And velvet draperies can impart.
Here is a symbol of a trust
Richer than wisdom thick with dust.

I see it through the half-swung door,
And smile to think long years before
I, too, on Christmas Eve was young
And eagerly a stocking hung
Beside the chimney just as she,
Ere knowledge stole my faith from me.

Upstairs about her bed there seems
The peace of childhood's lovely dreams,
And I, grown old, almost forget
The truths with which I am beset.

EDGAR GUEST

Glad Christmas bells are ringing,
And children's voices sweet
Mingle carols with their cadence
Bright Christmas Day to greet;
Bright Christmas Day to greet.
That brings us all good cheer.
Oh! our hearts chime to the music
Of bell tones sweet and clear.

The Christmas bells are ringing!
The world is full of cheer,
Oh! their sounds of joy and gladness
Give music to the ear—
Give music to the ear.
Those bells, dear bells of old!
Oh! my heart chimes to the music
By their glad tongues unrolled.

BARTLETT BURLEIGH JAMES

Here's to a happy holiday,
Health and wealth for all the year round!
Saint Nick will be back with reindeer and sleigh;
Let us sing and ring bells till the echoes resound.
We wish you a stocking with presents stuffed high,
And plenty of plums in your Christmas pie!

AUTHOR UNKNOWN

In the far-off Polar seas,
Far beyond the Hebrides,
Where the icebergs, towering high,
Seem to pierce the wintry sky,
And the fur-clad Esquimaux,
Glides in sledges o'er the snow,
Dwells St. Nick, the merry wight,
Patron saint of Christmas night.

Solid walls of massive ice,
Bearing many a quaint device,
Flanked by graceful turrets twain,
Clear as clearest porcelain,
Bearing at a lofty height
Christ's pure cross in simple white,
Carven with surpassing art
From an iceberg's crystal heart.

Here St. Nick, in royal state,
Dwells, until December late
Clips the days at either end,
And the nights at each extend;
Then, with his attendant sprites,
Scours the earth on wintry nights,
Bringing home, in well-filled hands,
Children's gifts from many lands.

Here are whistles, tops and toys,
Meant to gladden little boys;
Skates and sleds that soon will glide
O'er the ice or steep hill-side.
Here are dolls with flaxen curls,
Sure to charm the little girls;
Christmas books, with pictures gay,
For this welcome holiday.

In the court the reindeer wait,
Filled the sledge with costly freight.
As the first faint shadow falls,
Promptly from his icy halls
Steps St. Nick, and grasps the rein:
Straight his coursers scour the plain,
And afar, in measured time,
Sounds the sleigh-bells' silver chime.

Like an arrow from the bow
Speed the reindeer o'er the snow.
Onward! Now the loaded sleigh
Skirts the shores of Hudson's Bay.
Onward, till the stunted tree
Gains a loftier majesty,
And the curling smoke-wreaths rise
Under less inclement skies.

Built upon a hill-side steep
Lies a city wrapt in sleep.
Up and down the lonely street
Sleepy watchmen pace their beat.
Little heeds them Santa Claus;
Not for him are human laws.
With a leap he leaves the ground,
Scales the chimney at a bound.

Five small stockings hang below;
Five small stockings in a row.
From his pocket blithe St. Nick
Fills the waiting stockings quick;
Some with sweetmeats, some with toys,
Gifts for girls, and gifts for boys,
Mounts the chimney like a bird,
And the bells are once more heard.

Santa Claus! Good Christmas saint,
In whose heart no selfish taint
Findeth place, some homes there be
Where no stockings wait for thee,
Homes where sad young faces wear
Painful marks of Want and Care,
And the Christmas morning brings
No fair hope of better things.

Can you not some crumbs bestow
On these children steeped in woe;
Steal a single look of care
Which their sad young faces wear;
From your overflowing store
Give to them whose hearts are sore?
No sad eyes should greet the morn
When the infant Christ was born.

HORATIO ALGER
*"St. Nicholas"*

Everywhere, everywhere, Christmas to-night!
Christmas in lands of the fir tree and pine,
Christmas in lands of the palm tree and vine;
Christmas where snow peaks stand solemn and white,
Christmas where cornfields lie sunny and bright;
Everywhere, everywhere, Christmas to-night!

Christmas where children are hopeful and gay,
Christmas where old men are patient and gray;
Christmas where peace, like a dove in its flight;
Broods o'er brave men in the thick of the fight;
Everywhere, everywhere, Christmas to-night!

PHILLIPS BROOKS
*"Everywhere, Christmas To-Night"*

The best portion of a good man's life,
His little, nameless, unremembered acts,
Of kindness and of love.

WILLIAM WORDSWORTH

Good luck unto old Christmas,
And long life, let us sing,
For he doeth more good unto the poor
Than many a crowned king.

AUTHOR UNKNOWN

Over the River And Through the Woods...

...Now Grandmother's cap I spy.

D. Morgan©

*J*o was the first to wake in the gray dawn of Christmas morning. No stockings hung at the fireplace, and for a moment she felt as much disappointed as she did long ago, when her little sock fell down because it was crammed so full of goodies. Then she remembered her mother's promise and, slipping her hand under her pillow, drew out a little crimson-covered book. She knew it very well, for it was that beautiful old story of the best life ever lived, and Jo felt that it was a true guidebook for any pilgrim going on a long journey. She woke Meg with a "Merry Christmas," and bade her see what was under her pillow. A green-covered book appeared, with the same picture inside, and a few words written by their mother, which made their one present very precious in their eyes. Presently Beth and Amy woke to rummage and find their little books also, one dove-colored, the other blue, and all sat looking at and talking about them, while the east grew rosy with the coming day…

Not a very splendid show, but there was a great deal of love done up in the few little bundles, and the tall vase of red roses, white chrysanthemums, and trailing vines, which stood in the middle, gave quite an elegant air to the table.

"She's coming! Strike up, Beth! Open the door, Amy! Three cheers for Marmee!" cried Jo, prancing about while Meg went to conduct Mother to the seat of honor. Beth played her gayest march, Amy threw open the door, and Meg enacted escort with great dignity. Mrs. March was both surprised and touched, and smiled with her eyes full as she examined her presents and read the little notes which accompanied them. The slippers went on at once, a new handkerchief was slipped into her pocket, well scented with Amy's cologne, the rose was fastened in her bosom, and the nice gloves were pronounced a perfect fit.

There was a good deal of laughing and kissing and explaining, in the simple, loving fashion which makes these home festivals so pleasant at the time, so sweet to remember long afterward, and then all fell to work.

LOUISA MAY ALCOTT
*Little Women*

*God bless him! It was his first Christmas Eve,*
*and for hundreds of years since then he has nobly*
*fulfilled his mission to bring happiness to*
*the hearts of little children.*

L. FRANK BAUM

Dear Santa,
Are you still the same dear man I knew so long a

*Christmas is not only the mile-mark of another year, moving us to*
*thoughts of self-examination: it is a season, from all its associations,*
*whether domestic or religious, suggesting thoughts of joy.*

ROBERT LOUIS STEVENSON

*A kind heart is a fountain of gladness,*
*making everything in its vicinity*
*fresben into smiles.*

WASHINGTON IRVING

*Does Mrs. Claus still mend your suit............*

*and pack your bag to go?*

D. Morgan

*Kindness in words creates confidence.*
*Kindness in thinking creates profoundness.*
*Kindness in giving creates love.*

LAO TZU

# Father Christmas Around the World

| | |
|---|---|
| United States: | Santa Claus |
| England: | Father Christmas |
| France: | Père Noël |
| Germany: | Klaasbuur |
| Belgium: | Sint Niklaas |
| Netherlands: | Sinterklaas |
| Spain: | San Nicolás |
| Italy: | Babbo Natale |
| Poland: | Sw. Mikolaj |
| Germany: | der Weihnachtsmann |
| Russia: | Dyed Moroz |
| Japanese: | Santa Krosu |

*It is all very well to praise the rest,*
*But I love the merry Christmas best,*
*For it makes me think of a mother mild,*
*Of a manger, a star and a little Child,*
*Of angels that sang above the earth*
*On the holy night of our Saviour's birth;*
*And then besides, there are Christmas trees,*
*And brimful stockings, and more than these,*
*Cakes and candies, and nuts and toys*
*For all the good little girls and boys.*
*Christmas, then, is the day for me,*
*With its peace and love and its jollity.*

"National Holidays"
*The Sunshine Reader, 1888*

*With every step ..... through watchful care ... we have a guardian angel there.*

Four little feet pattering on the floor,
Two tangled curly heads peeping at the door;
Hear the merry laughter, happy, childish
Early Christmas morning.

Two little stockings full of sweets and toys,
Everything charming for little girls and boys.
How could they help then, making such a noise?
Early Christmas morning.

Down beside the stockings, many gifts were spread,
Dollies, drums, a cradle, and a brand new sled.
"Haven't we too many?" little Nellie said,
Early Christmas morning.

"Yes," says John to Nellie, as he spied the two,
"We've so many presents, tell you what
I'll give half of mine away. Now, dear Nell, will you?"
Early Christmas morning.

Two little famished ones in the house were called,
Favors heaped upon them till they stood enthralled.
Was not this the angel's song, "Peace, good will to all?"
Early Christmas morning.

"EARLY CHRISTMAS MORNING"
*The Sunshine Reader, 1888*

It was a pretty sight, and a seasonable one, that met their eyes when they flung the door open. In the fore-court, lit by the dim rays of a horn lantern, some eight or ten little field-mice stood in a semicircle, red worsted comforters round their throats, their fore-paws thrust deep into their pockets, their feet jigging for warmth. With bright beady eyes they glanced shyly at each other, sniggering a little, sniffing and applying coat-sleeves a good deal. As the door opened, one of the elder ones that carried the lantern was just saying, "Now then, one, two, three!" and forthwith their shrill little voices uprose on the air, singing one of the old-time carols that their forefathers composed in fields that were fallow and held by frost, or when snow-bound in chimney corners, and handed down to be sung in the miry street to lamp-lit windows at Yule-time.

### CAROL

*Villagers all, this frosty tide,*
*Let your doors swing open wide,*
*Though wind may follow, and snow beside,*
*Yet draw us in by your fire to bide;*
*Joy shall be yours in the morning!*
*Here we stand in the cold and the sleet,*
*Blowing fingers and stamping feet,*
*Come from far away you to greet—*
*You by the fire and we in the street—*
*Bidding you joy in the morning!*
*For ere one half of the night was gone,*
*Sudden a star has led us on,*
*Raining bliss and benison—*
*Bliss to-morrow and more anon,*
*Joy for every morning!*

Kenneth Grahame
*The Wind in the Willows*

**O**f all the old festivals, however, that of Christmas awakens the strongest and most heartfelt associations. There is a tone of solemn and sacred feeling that blends with our conviviality, and lifts the spirit to a state of hallowed and elevated enjoyment. The services of the church about this season are extremely tender and inspiring. They dwell on the beautiful story of the origin of our faith, and the pastoral scenes that accompanied its announcement. They gradually increase in fervor and pathos during the season of Advent, until they break forth in full jubilee on the morning that brought peace and good-will to men. I do not know a grander effect of music on the moral feelings, than to hear the full choir and the pealing organ performing a Christmas anthem in a cathedral, and filling every part of the vast pile with triumphant harmony.

It is a beautiful arrangement, also, derived from days of yore, that this festival, which commemorates the announcement of the religion of peace and love, has been made the season for gathering together of family connections, and drawing closer again those bands of kindred hearts, which the cares and pleasures and sorrows of the world are continually operating to cast loose; of calling back the children of a family, who have launched forth in life, and wandered widely asunder, once more to assemble about the paternal hearth, that rallying place of the affections, there to grow young and loving again among the endearing mementos of childhood.

WASHINGTON IRVING
*Christmas*

He was round as an apple, with a fresh rosy face,
laughing eyes, and a bushy beard as white as snow. A
red cloak trimmed with beautiful ermine hung from
his shoulders and upon his back was a basket filled
with pretty presents for the Princess Ozma.
"Hello, Dorothy; still having adventures?"
he asked in his jolly way, as he took
the girl's hand in both his own.
"How did you know my name, Santa?" she replied,
feeling more shy in the presence of this immortal saint
than she ever had before in her young life.
"Why, don't I see you every Christmas Eve, when
you're asleep?" he rejoined, pinching her blushing cheek.

L. FRANK BAUM
The Road to Oz

Saint Nicholas, holy man and good,
Put on your cloak, put on your hood;
Hasten to Amsterdam, and again
From Amsterdam go into Spain,
There the apples big and sweet
Grown in Orange, roll the street;
Grown in Orange and Granada
Under sun and under shadow.
Oh, Saint Nicholas, my good friend,
I have served thee without end,
If my wish thou'lt now give me,
I'll devote my life to thee.

OLD FLEMISH HYMN SUNG BY CHILDREN
AT CHRISTMASTIME

The only gift is a portion of thyself.

RALPH WALDO EMERSON

What can I give Him,
Poor as I am?
If I were a shepherd
I would bring a lamb,
If I were a wise man
I would do my part
Yet what can I give Him?
Give my heart.

CHRISTINA ROSETTI

41

A rattle at the little old window made everybody look there, just as a great snow-white head popped up over the sill...

"He's a-comin' in!" cried Davie in chorus, which sent Phronsie flying to Polly. In jumped a little old man, quite spry for his years; with a jolly, red face and a pack on his back, and flew into their midst, prepared to do his duty; but what should he do, instead of making his speech, "this jolly Old Saint"— but first fly up to Mrs. Pepper, and say— "Oh, mammy, how did you do it?"

Margaret Sidney
*Five Little Peppers and How They Grew*

*Christmas, the time of year that has the impact*
*of a childhood story and the dreams of the future*
*all rolled into the present that we give our loved ones.*
*Christmas may be many things or it may be a few.*
*For you, the joy is each new toy; for me, it's watching you.*

JOSEPH KALLINGER
*Past and Present*

*Every action of our lives touches on some chord*
*that will vibrate in eternity.*

Edwin Hubbel Chapin

At Christmas—the season
Of giving and sharing,
Of living and loving
Remembering, caring—
Our thoughts bridge the space that
Would tend to divide us
Restoring the warmth of
Your presence beside us.
May all the sweet magic
Of Christmas conspire
To gladden your hearts
And fill every desire.

HAROLD H. BENN

*Be charitable and indulgent to everyone but thyself.*

JOSEPH JOBBER

*Christmas, my child, is love in action.*
*Every time we love, every time we give,*
*it's Christmas.*

DALE EVANS ROGERS